PARKER'S PEEK-A-BOO MOON
Written by Angel Anderson
Illustrations by B. Robbins

Dedicated to my Grandson Parker who was my inspiration for this storybook.

Self-Published by
Angel Anderson

This is a story about a boy named Parker who is very fascinated by the moon and shares his passion for the moon with his Grandma.

Parker was used to staying home with his mom. Then, one day his mom had good news. She told Parker, “I got a new job! Now you will be going to see your Grandma 3 days a week after school.”

This news made Parker happy because he and his Grandma love looking at the moon together.

Parker was excited to go to his Grandma's house because she always took him for walks, no matter what the weather was like.

After they ate dinner Parker and his Grandma set out for their walk.

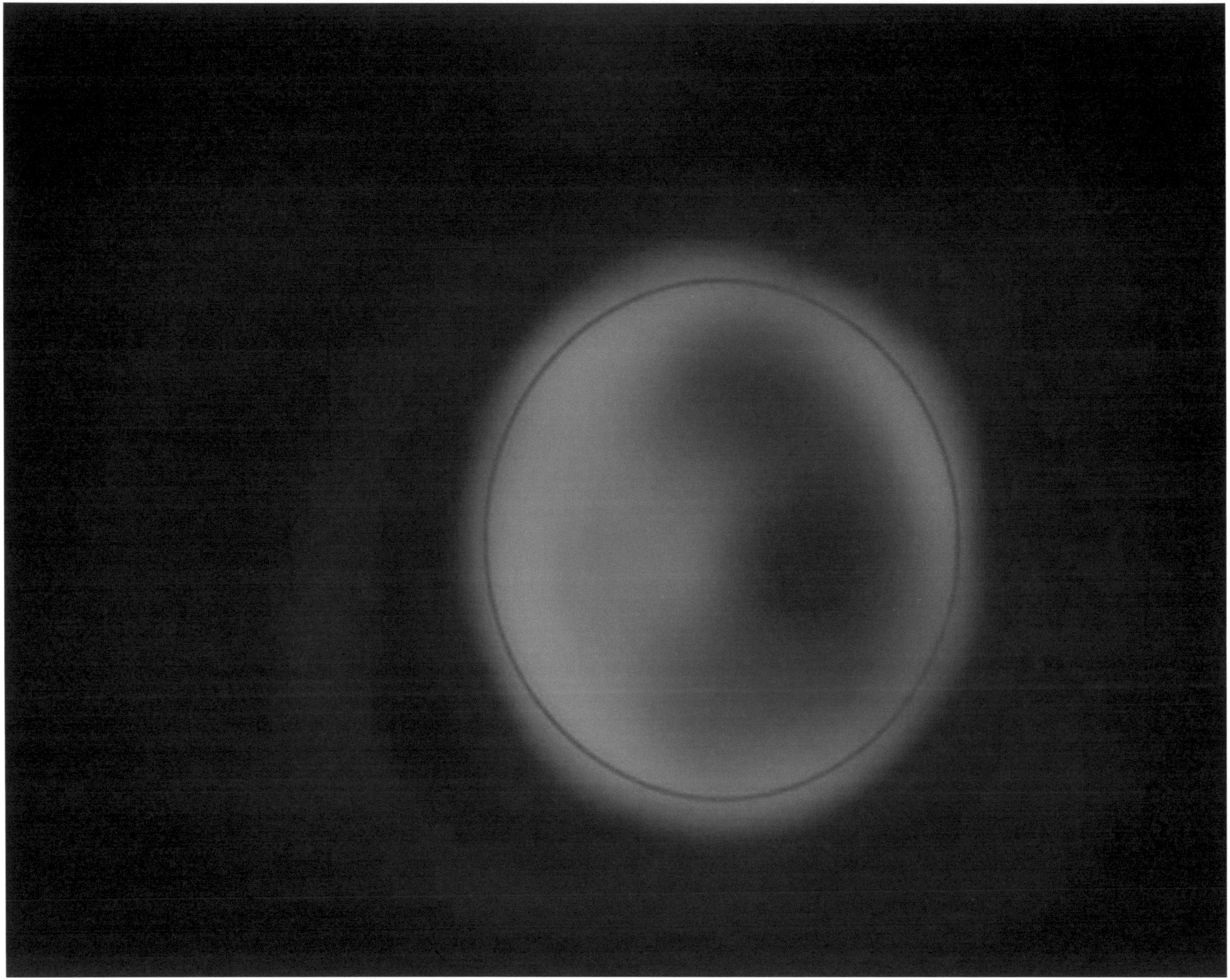

As they were walking, Parker looked up and said, “Grandma look at the moon. It is so BIG!”

“Yes, it is,” his Grandma said. “That is a full moon!”

As Parker and his Grandma walked back home, Parker looked up in the sky again.

“Hey Grandma, Where is the moon, is it gone?” Parker asked.

“No it’s not silly, it’s playing Peek-A-Boo with you!” As they walked a little further, his Grandma said, “There it is Parker, see there it is behind the tree!”

“Oh, there it is, I see it now!

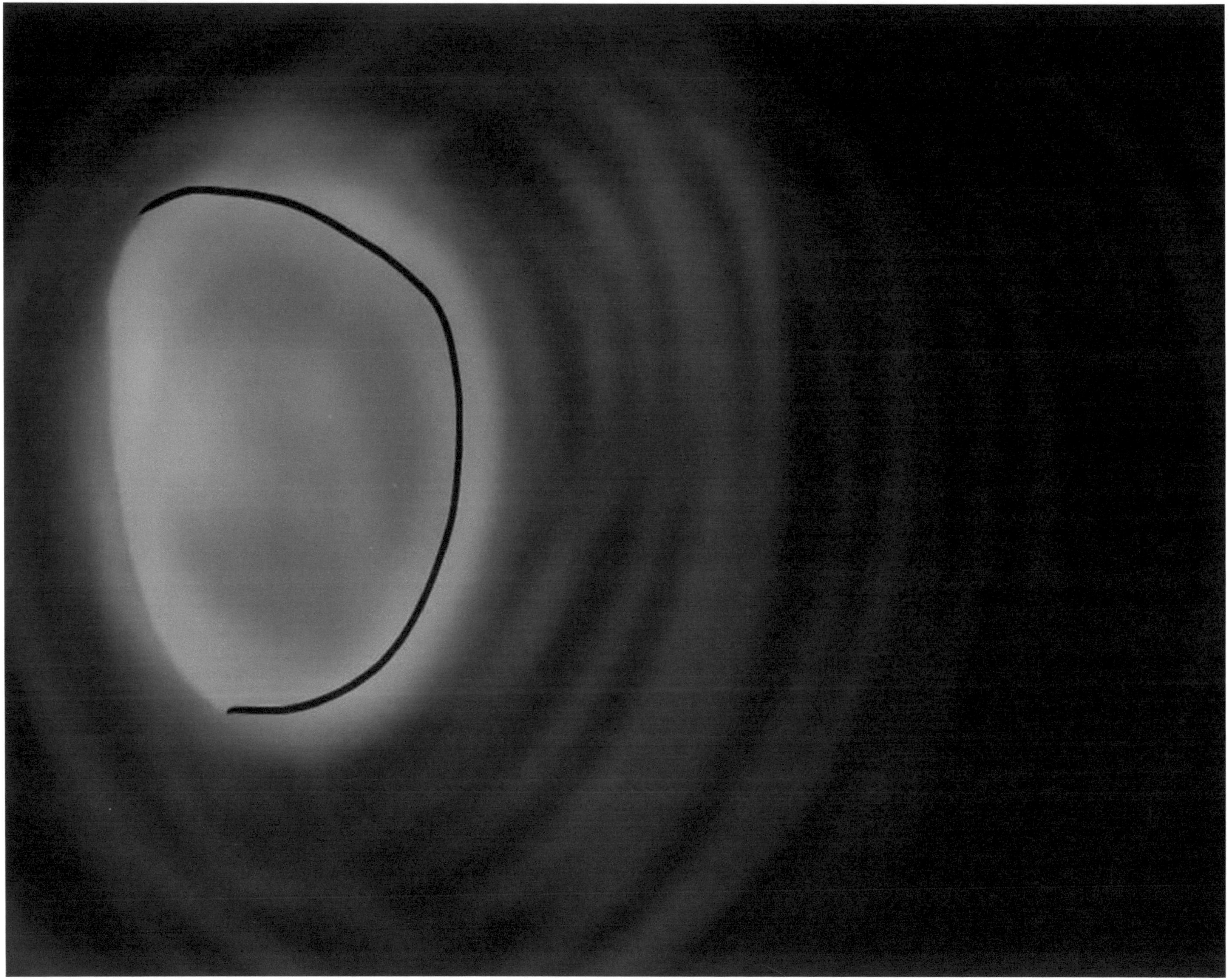

The next time Parker and his Grandma were out on their walk, Parker said, “Hey Grandma, what happened to the moon? It looks like somebody took a bite out of it!”

His Grandma smiled down at him and said, “Parker, when the moon looks like that it is called a Waning Gibbous Moon. The moon changes phases about every 3 days.”

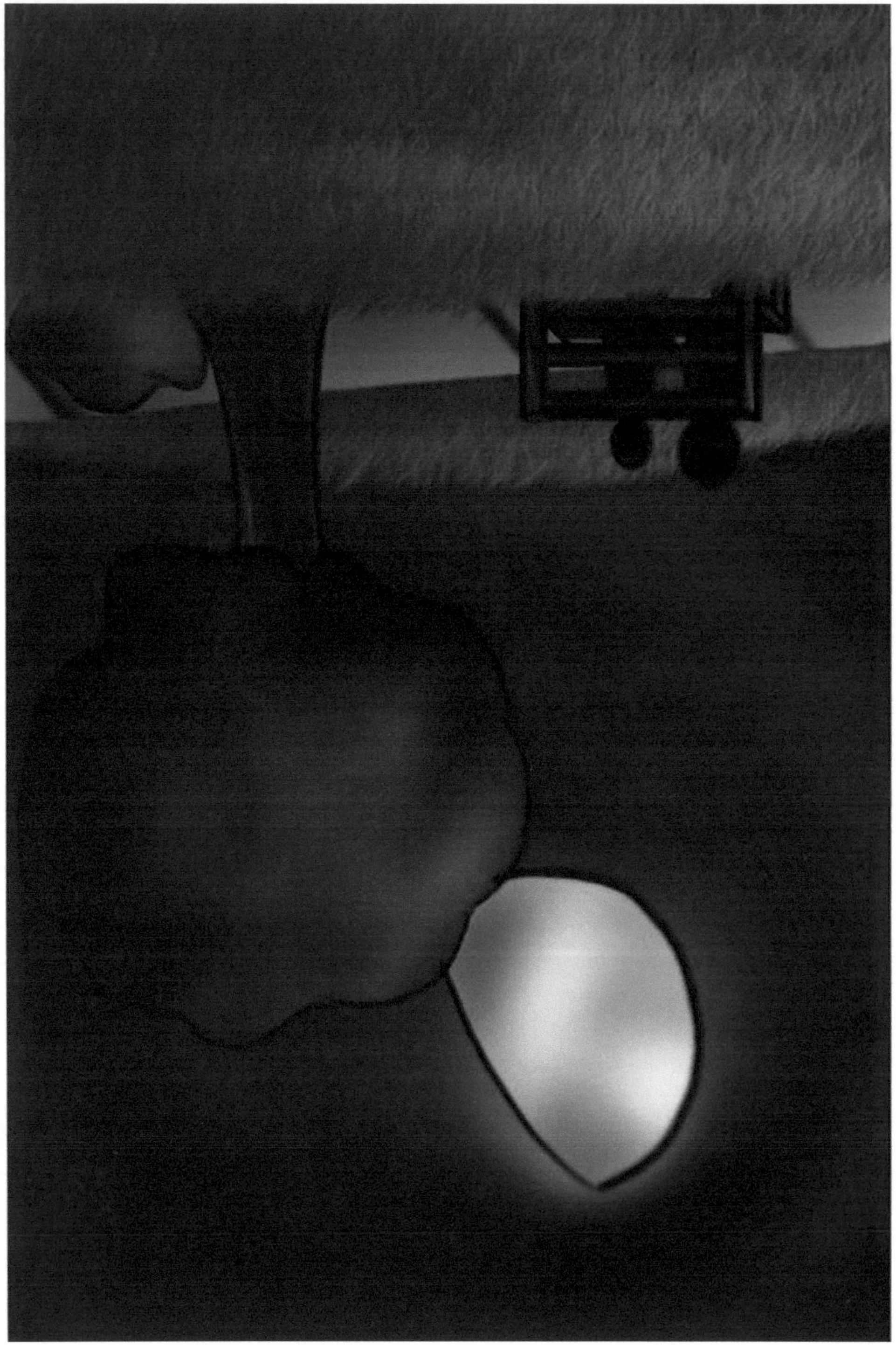

A few days later, while taking their after dinner walk, Parker looked up at the moon and could not believe what he saw.

Parker said, “Grandma, now someone took a bigger bite out of the moon!”

“Remember,” Grandma said, “we talked about the moon changing. This is called the Last Quarter Moon.”

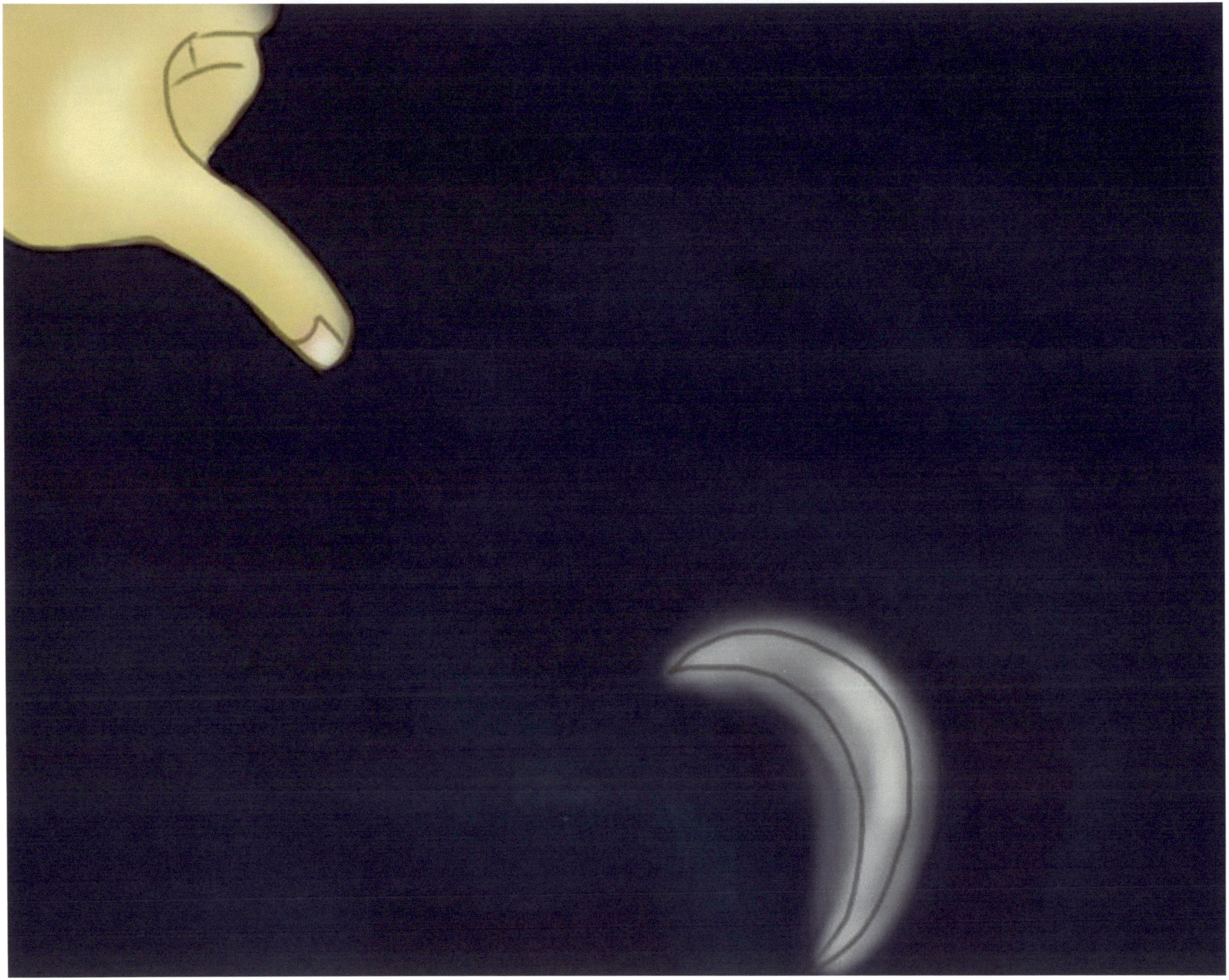

Then one night, coming home from an evening walk, Parker looked up. To his amazement, the moon looked like it was smiling sideways at him. He excitedly said, “Look at the moon now Grandma!”

His Grandma replied, “It’s beautiful, Parker. It is called a Waning Crescent Moon.”

"Let's go see the moon, Parker. Tonight the moon is going to be different," Grandma said, after they finished eating dinner.

"Why, Grandma?" Parker asked.

"Come on, you will see!" Grandma replied excitedly.

As they walked, Parker looked up and asked, "Grandma, what happened to the light of the moon?"

"That moon is called a new moon," Grandma explained. "We can't see the lighted side when we have a new moon. But as always, in a few days it will change."

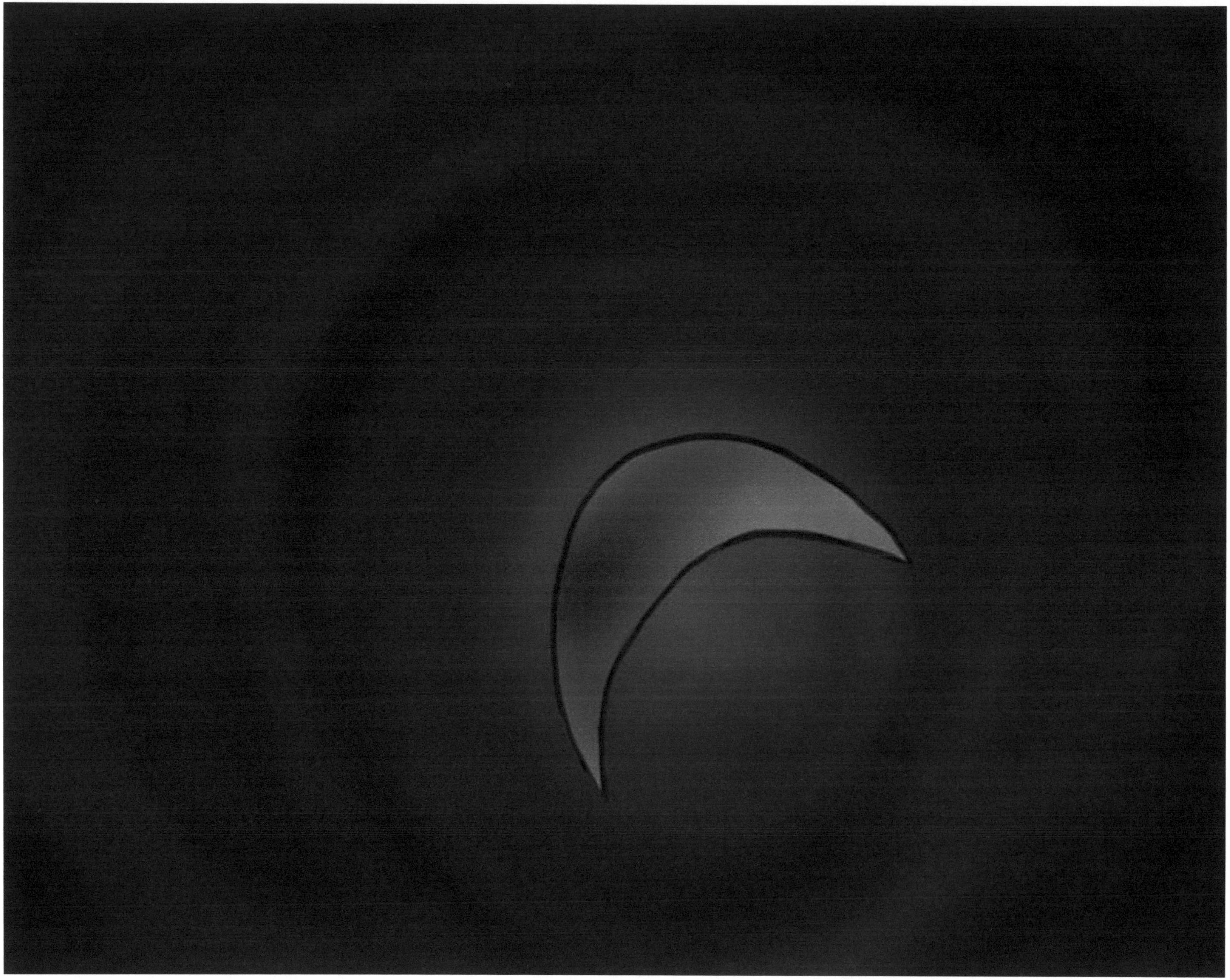

Parker could not wait for his next visit with his Grandma. While out walking, he looked up at the moon. “Look! You were right, Grandma! The light is coming back in the moon!” Parker said with excitement.

“It’s beautiful. That is called the Waxing Crescent Moon, Parker.” His Grandma continued, “The moon is on its way back to being a Full Moon again.”

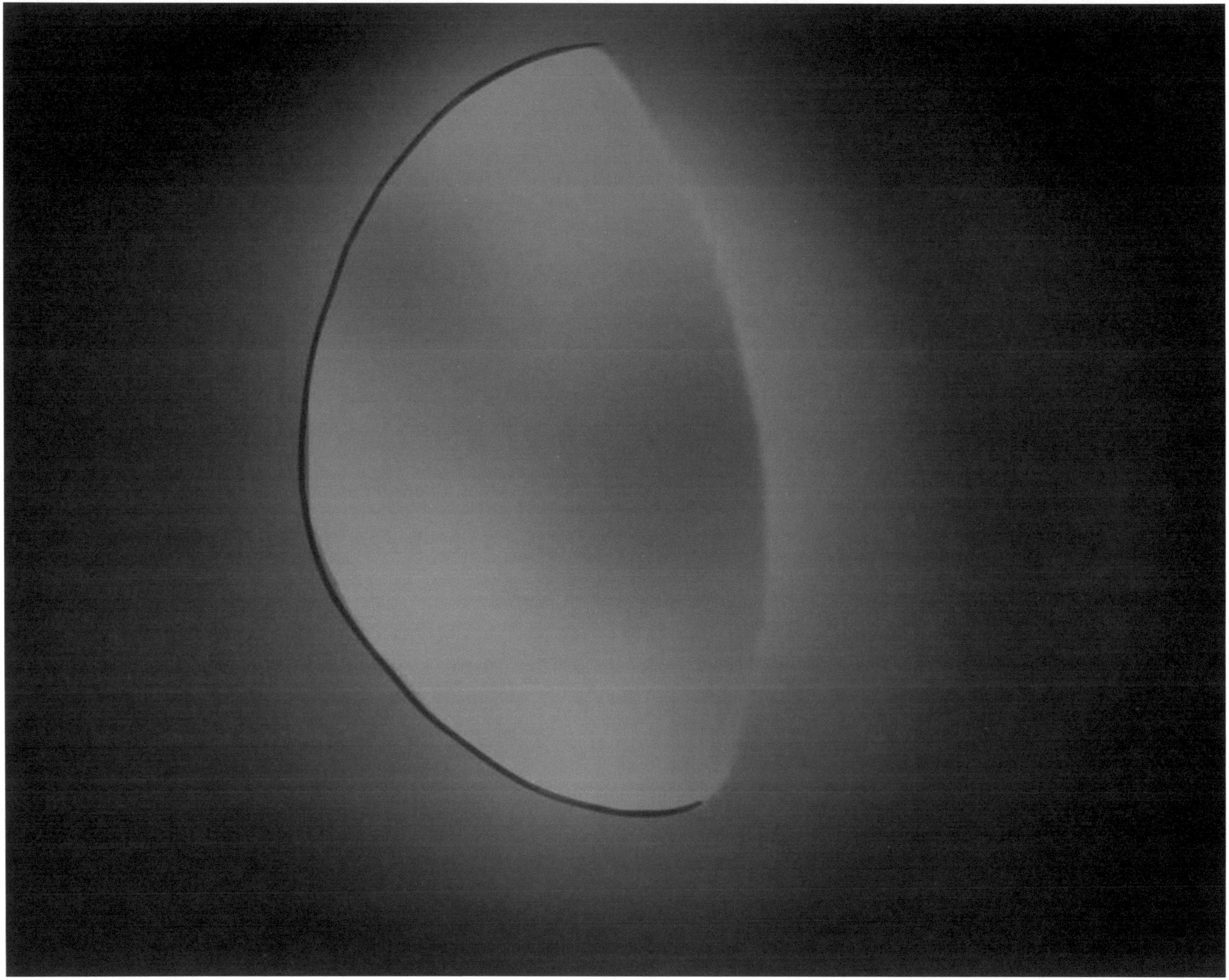

Parker was beginning to remember the moons he saw, for on his next walk, he said “Look, Grandma it’s a half moon again! We saw this moon before, didn’t we Grandma?” he asked.

“Well, Parker, we saw a similar moon” his Grandma answered. “This one is called the First Quarter Moon because the light is on the right side of the moon.”

"Grandma, the moon looks so far away today," Parker noticed.

"It does. Do you want to know what that one is called?" his Grandma asked.

"Yes!" Parker said excitedly.

"It is the Waxing Gibbous Moon. It is the last moon before the Full Moon."

One day during an evening walk, he asked, “Grandma, how do you know so much about the moon?”

“Well, Parker, I read a lot of books. When we get back to my house, I will show you a book that has a chart of the moons to help you understand more.”

All about
#1

"Parker, look at this page. It shows all the phases of the moon," his Grandma said.

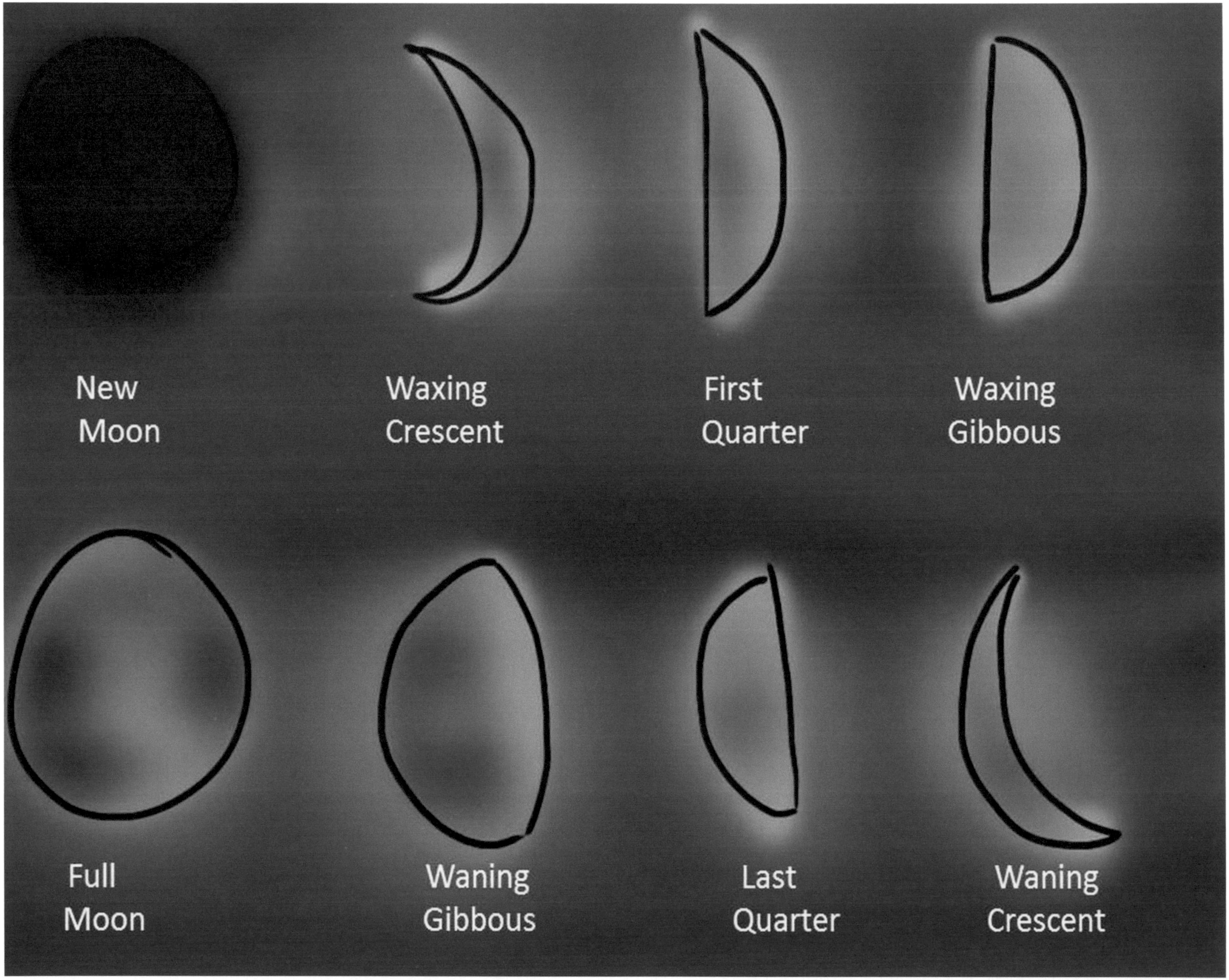
New Moon
Waxing Crescent
First Quarter
Waxing Gibbous
Full Moon
Waning Gibbous
Last Quarter
Waning Crescent

Grandma asked Parker, “After seeing these pictures of the moon, do you understand better now?”

“I do, Grandma. Thank you so much!”

"Grandma," Parker said, while looking out the window, "when I grow up, I want to be as smart as you! Thank you for teaching me about the moon. Now I can be an astronaut!"

"You are welcome, I love you! You are so cute. Remember you can be anything you want to be!"

"I Love You Too Grandma!"

THE END

ABOUT THE AUTHOR

Ms. Anderson is from Portland, Oregon. When she is not writing, she enjoys spending time with her Grandchildren.

Parker's Peek-A-Boo Moon is her first published children's book. Look for more children's books to be published in the near future.

A Note From The Author

"I want to thank my family, friends and all of those who have supported me throughout this adventure."

"Thank you for your purchase. Please visit my Facebook page at: https://www.facebook.com/AngelAndersonAuthorPage"

Additional copies available at Amazon.com

PARKER'S PEEK-A-BOO MOON

Parker's Peek-a-Boo Moon is an educational children's book. A great way to read to your children while teaching them about the moon.

www.ingramcontent.com/pod-product-compliance
Lightning Source LLC
Chambersburg PA
CBHW041237040426
42445CB00004B/53
* 9 7 8 0 6 1 5 8 0 4 2 4 8 *